HANNAH
AND THE
LOST JELLY SHOE

A TRUE STORY OF FAITH

WRITTEN BY
CARLIE TERRADEZ

ILLUSTRATED BY
MICHAEL VALLADO

Published by Harrison House Publishers
Shippensburg, PA 17257

Cover and Interior artwork by Michael Vallado
Michael Learns Art, LLC, Los Angeles, CA
www.michaellearnsart.com

ISBN 13 HC: 978-1-6675-0295-3
ISBN 13 eBook: 978-1-6675-0296-0

For Worldwide Distribution, Printed in India.
1 2 3 4 5 6 7 8 / 30 29 28 27 26 25 24 23

HANNAH
AND THE
LOST JELLY SHOE

This Book Belongs to:

_____

_____

The kids gathered around Mum as she read from the Bible. Zach and Josh were paying attention, but Hannah was daydreaming.

Mum paused, "Hannah, are you listening?"

Hannah startled and turned from the window.

"Sorry, Mum! I'm just excited about our trip to the beach tomorrow!"

2

Mum shook her head with a smile and continued to read from the Bible.

"Give all your worries to Him, because He cares for you."

Hannah tilted her head and asked, "How do we give our worries to Jesus, Mum?"

Josh hopped to his feet, grabbed a nearby toy, and hurled it to the ground.

"You pick 'em up and smash 'em down right in Jesus' lap!"

4

Mum and Hannah laughed while Zach shook his head at his little brother's antics.

"No, silly," Zach replied. "You can't pick up your worries! You just tell Jesus about them and let Him take care of them."

Hannah looked at Mum, waiting for her to have the final say.

"Both of you are right! If something happens that makes you worried or sad, you should take some time to pray."

"If you hold on to your worries, they can hurt you.

It's like holding on to a prickly cactus!

So, throw them to Jesus quick because He won't get hurt."

"Jesus loves you so much. He will always take care of the things that concern you."

"Anything we worry about?" Hannah asked.

"Well, this verse says to give all your worries to Him. So that means everything: big and small!" Mum explained.

"Now it's time for bed!"

As the boys scurried off to their beds, Hannah prayed. "Thank You for caring about me, Jesus. Even about the little things!"

And Hannah peacefully drifted off to sleep.

The next day, Hannah raced over the sand toward the ocean.

Her big brothers were faster, but she wasn't too far behind!

The boys kicked off their sandals
before they reached the water, but
Hannah didn't want to take off her
favorite pair of blue jelly shoes.

She loved the dolphin on the sole
that left prints in the sand
behind her as she ran.

11

Hannah and her family played for hours!

They had splash battles,

played catch,

built sandcastles,

and ate a picnic lunch.

They were having a wonderful time, until...

As the children swam, one of Hannah's
jelly shoes slipped off her foot.

"Oh, no!" Hannah cried in dismay.
"Where's Jelly? I've lost one of my shoes!"

The whole family searched for the precious shoe.

Dad swam out into deeper water.

14

Zach put on a snorkel to search while Josh kicked around and dug in the sand nearby.

Mum and Hannah walked up and down the shoreline to see if Jelly had washed up.

But Jelly was nowhere to be found!

Mum frowned. They had only packed one pair of shoes for Hannah.

Knowing that this missing shoe was her favorite,

Mum worried Hannah would be upset.

Hannah's eyes began to fill with tears. But then she remembered the Bible verse Mum had read to them the night before:

"Give all your worries to Him, because He cares for you."

Then Hannah knew in her heart that even though Jelly was lost, Jesus would find the shoe.

Jesus cares about the little things, even my lost Jelly, she thought. Hannah wiped her eyes and said with confident faith,

"Jelly will come back, in Jesus' name!"

Mum and Dad weren't quite as sure that Jelly would reappear. They were on a mission to find Hannah a new pair of shoes.

She couldn't just wear one shoe for the rest of the trip...

...could she?

After packing up their beach gear, they went to town and searched every store for a pair of size six shoes.

But there was not a single pair that would fit!

21

Hannah happily wore her single blue jelly shoe.

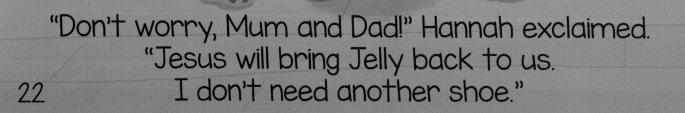

"Don't worry, Mum and Dad!" Hannah exclaimed.
"Jesus will bring Jelly back to us.
I don't need another shoe."

Hannah's faith encouraged Mum and Dad. They decided to stop trying to find new shoes.

Dad said, "Okay, Hannah. We won't worry about Jelly anymore."

"That's right," Mum agreed. "We are giving this worry to Jesus!"

23

Zach nodded. "We're not gonna hold on to it."

"Yeah!" Josh chimed in. "We don't want
it to prick us like a cactus!"

Dad suggested ice cream. With a cheer, the family left the shoe shopping, and their worry, behind.

That night, as Hannah drifted off to sleep, she wondered what adventures Jelly might be having...

26

27

28

30

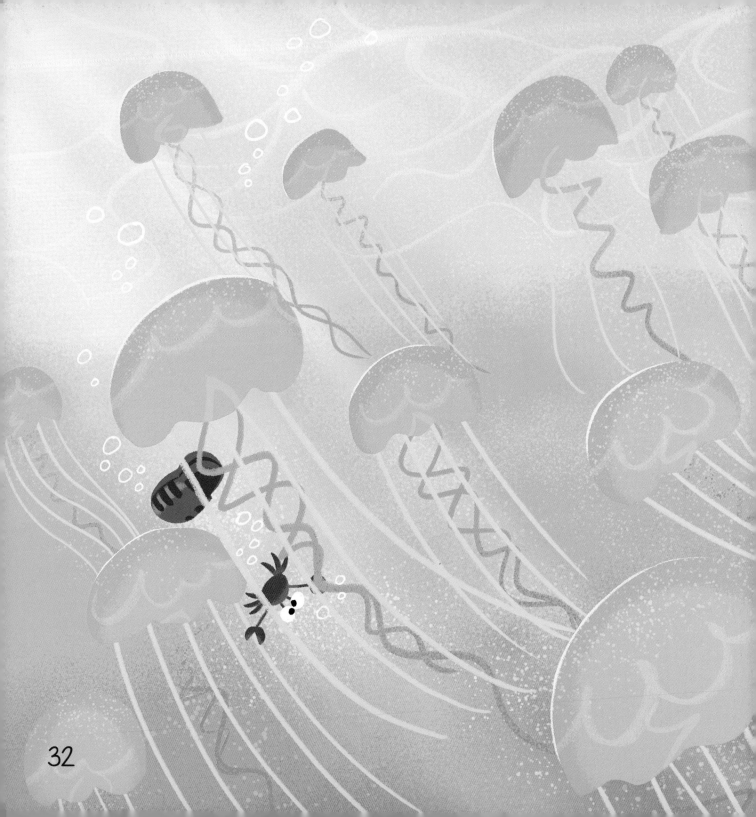

33

The next morning, Hannah and her family returned to the beach.

Hannah knew that Jesus would bring Jelly back.

So, she was focused on having fun!

As they walked to the same spot as the day before, a tiny bit of blue caught Hannah's eye.

She squealed with excitement!

Hannah ran across the sand with a grin as her curious family trailed behind.

35

Hannah tugged Jelly out of the sand. With a giggle, she slipped Jelly onto her bare foot and fastened the rusty buckle.

"This one has been on an adventure!" Hannah exclaimed.

36

Impossibly, Jelly had come back out of the sea and was waiting exactly where the family had been playing the day before!

"I knew Jesus would bring Jelly back."
Hannah beamed at her family. "Thank you
for believing it, too!"

"Hannah, you showed us how to give our
worries to Jesus," Dad said with a proud smile.

"Yeah, Jesus caught our worry about Jelly so it wouldn't hurt us."

"He really does care, even about little things!"

"Thank You, Lord, for bringing Jelly back," Mum prayed.

39

Things will happen that you don't expect.
You might feel upset or worried. But Jesus
wants you to give all of your cares to Him!

He loves you, and He cares about
what you care about.

Even the little things.

"Give all your worries to Him,
because He cares for you."

I Peter 5:7 ICB

Hannah's Healing

From the time Hannah was born, she suffered from a rare auto-immune disease, eosinophilic enteropathy, which caused her body to reject any food she would try to eat. Doctors tried several extreme methods to overcome her disease, including surgically inserting a feeding tube. By the time Hannah was three years old, all methods to feed her had failed, and she was dying. So her parents, Ashley and Carlie, removed Hannah from the hospital and went to a conference to find someone who would agree with them in faith for her healing.

Hannah & Mum, 2019

On March 18, 2006, Andrew Wommack prayed for Hannah in Jesus' name. **That day, Hannah was supernaturally healed and able to eat anything she wanted!** You can watch Hannah's complete healing testimony on our website at TerradezMinistries.com/about/.

Miracles & Healing Made Easy records Hannah's healing testimony in even more detail. Carlie also tells of how she was healed of paralysis and epilepsy, and other powerful testimonies. This book will inspire you as you experience accounts of miracles in the lives of everyday believers!

Available wherever books are sold

To learn more about Hannah and Carlie's healing testimonies, access hours of free teaching materials, or contact our ministry, please visit our website at Terradez.com.

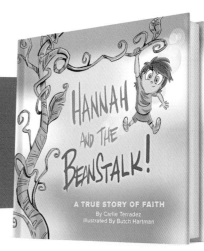

Ashley & Carlie Terradez

Ashley and Carlie Terradez are international speakers, authors, and ministry leaders who are passionate about empowering the body of Christ to walk in the full abundance of the Gospel.

After their three-year-old daughter, Hannah, was miraculously healed of a deadly auto-immune disease, Ashley and Carlie knew they were called to share God's abundant goodness with the world.

After graduating from Bible college in the UK in 2008, they followed the call of God to the United States with their three children. They were ordained in 2011 and founded Terradez Ministries shortly thereafter with a mandate to empower believers in the promises of God.

FREE Confession Card

Declare God's Word Over Your Life!

The most powerful scriptures from God's Word, declaring who you are in Christ, can all be found in one place: the Terradez Ministries' Confession Card! In this colorful, fun, "prescription-sized" confession card, you will speak out your true identity in Christ daily! As you speak God's Word over yourself it will soon become a living reality.

Scan me

To receive your FREE Confession Card, scan this QR code or visit Terradez.com/confession-card.